COMFY AND COZY CROCHET BLANKETS

SARAH THOMPSON

RICHTEXTURESCROCHET.COM

FOR MY CHILDREN WHO LOVE A COMFY AND COZY BLANKET!

TABLE OF CONTENTS

RICHTEXTURESCROCHET.COM

TABLE OF CONTENTS CONTINUED...

RICHTEXTURESCROCHET.COM

INTRODUCTION

LEARN TO CROCHET FIVE COMFY AND COZY CROCHET BLANKETS!

Cozy blankets are a staple in my home. At any given time you will find a couple tossed over the back of a couch. They are kept handy for when company arrives or for when a day or night is especially cold during the winter months.

In this little booklet you will find six plush and cozy crochet blankets. Each blanket features its own unique texture and colour scheme.

These blankets are all reversible! This means that when they are on display, there is no need to adjust them so that the front is showing. Enjoy!

It is my hope that these crochet blankets will inspire and bring cozy comfort to your home and the homes of the people you love and care for.

Happy Crocheting!

Sarah Thompson

MATERIALS AND TOOLS

Yarn:

Each of the crochet patterns in this book was completed using a jumbo weight (7) yarn called Sweet Snuggles ™ by Loops & Threads ®.

Sweet Snuggles ™ is a soft, 100% polyester yarn that is available in a variety of earth and jewel tones. Exact amounts and colours will be given at the start of each pattern.

You may, however, use your favourite jumbo weight yarn for this project. You may also use a favourite yarn fibre, although I do recommend a yarn type that is durable and easy to wash.

Hook:

For these crochet patterns, you will need a 10 mm (N/P/15) crochet hook. You may change the size of your crochet hook as needed to obtain the correct gauge.

Remember, if you make any changes to the yarn or hook, you may also need to adjust the amount of yarn used in each project.

Notions:

Along with your yarn and hook it may be helpful to have a pair of scissors, yarn needle, and measuring tape on hand. Supplies for blocking your completed blanket are optional (Due to the thickness of the yarn I didn't not block my finished blankets!)

CROCHET PATTERNS

BIG BOBBLE BLANKET 

Intermediate / Intermédiaire / Intermedio

MATERIALS AND INFORMATION

Gauge: 6 sts x 4 rows of dc = 4 inches

Finished Size: Approximately 47 x 52 inches

Yarn: Sweet Snuggles ™ by Loops & Threads ® (100% Polyester; 250 g/8.8 oz; Approx. 109 yds/100 meters). Jumbo (7). Colours Shown: Teal (colour A), Black (colour B) and Winter White (colour C). You will need 6 balls of colour A, 3 balls of colour B, 3 balls colour C; about 12 balls/1300 yds in total.

Hook: Size N/P 15 (10.0 mm) Hook. Adjust hook size if necessary to obtain correct gauge.

Notions: Yarn Needle

PATTERN NOTES

- Pattern is written in American English terms.
- Pattern is worked in rows.
- Ch 1 at beginning of row does not count as a stitch.
- Ch 2 at beginning of row does not count as a stitch.
- Ch 3 at beginning of row counts as a double crochet stitch.
- Weave in ends as needed.
- At the end of each section of colour, fasten off the previous colour an weave in your ends.
- To change the size of your blanket you will need a multiple of 4 stitches, plus 3 and then add 2 more stitches for your foundation chain.

STITCHES AND ABBREVIATIONS

Bobble: Bobble Stitch ([yo, insert your hook in the indicated st, yo and draw up a loop, yo and draw through 2 loops] 5 times, yo and draw through all the remaining loops on your hook. Bobble Stitch made.

Bpdc - Back Post Double Crochet

Ch – Chain

Dc - Double Crochet

Fpdc - Front Post Double Crochet

Hdc - Half Double Crochet

Rpt – Repeat

Sc - Single Crochet

Sk - Skip

Sl St – Slip Stitch

Yo – Yarn Over

PATTERN:

With colour A, Ch 73.

Row 1: Dc in the 4th ch from your hook and in each ch across. Ch 1, turn. (71 sts here and throughout)

Row 2: Hdc in the 1st st, * fpdc around the next st, bpdc around the next st; Rpt from * across to the last st, hdc in the top of the turning chain. Ch 1, turn.

Row 3: Hdc in the 1st st, * bpdc around the next st, fpdc around the next st; Rpt from * across to the last st, hdc in the top of the turning chain. Ch 1, turn.

Row 4: Hdc in the 1st st, * fpdc around the next st, bpdc around the next st; Rpt from * across to the last st, hdc in the top of the turning chain. Ch 2 (does not count as a st), turn.

Row 5: Dc in the 1st st and in each st across. Ch 2, turn.

Row 6: Dc in the 1st st and in each st across. Ch 1, turn.

Row 7: Sc in the 1st 3 sts *bobble (see "stitches and abbreviations") in the next st, sc in each of the next 3 sts; Rpt from * across. Ch 2, turn.

Row 8: Dc in the 1st st and in each st across. Ch 2, turn.

Row 9: Dc in the 1st st and in each st across. Switch to colour B in the final st. With colour B, ch 2, turn.

Rows 10 - 14: With colour B, repeat rows 5-9 switching to colour C at the end of row 14.

Rows 15 - 19: With colour C, repeat rows 5-9 switching to colour A at the end of row 19.

Rows 20 - 24: With colour A, repeat rows 5-9 switching to colour B at the end of row 24.

Continued...

PATTERN CONTINUED:

Rows 25 - 29: With colour B, repeat rows 5-9 switching to colour C at the end of row 29.

Rows 30 - 34: With colour C, repeat rows 5-9 switching to colour A at the end of row 34.

Rows 35 - 39: With colour A, repeat rows 5-9, continue working in colour A.

Row 40: Dc in the 1st st and in each st across. Ch 1, turn.

Row 41: Hdc in the 1st st, * fpdc around the next st, bpdc around the next st; Rpt from * across to the last st, hdc in the top of the turning chain. Ch 1, turn.

Row 42: Hdc in the 1st st, * bpdc around the next st, fpdc around the next st; Rpt from * across to the last st, hdc in the top of the turning chain. Ch 1, turn.

Row 43: Hdc in the 1st st, * fpdc around the next st, bpdc around the next st; Rpt from * across to the last st, hdc in the top of the turning chain.

Fasten off, weave in your ends.

DENIM STRIPES BLANKET

MATERIALS AND INFORMATION

Skill Level: Easy

Gauge: 8 sts x 7 rows of moss stitch = 4 inches

Finished Size: 49 x 38 inches

Yarn: Sweet Snuggles ™ by Loops & Threads ® (100% Polyester; 250 g/8.8 oz; Approx. 109 yds/100 meters). Jumbo (7). Colours Shown: Denim (colour A), Chalk Blue (Colour B). You will need 5 balls of colour A, 1 ball of colour B; 654 yds in total.

Hook: Size N/P 15 (10.0 mm) Hook. Adjust hook size if necessary to obtain correct gauge.

Notions: Yarn Needle

PATTERN NOTES

- Pattern is written in American English terms.
- Pattern is worked in rows.
- Ch 1 at beginning of row does not count as a stitch.
- Ch 2 at beginning of row does not count as a stitch.
- Ch 3 at beginning of row counts as a double crochet stitch.
- Weave in ends as needed.
- At the end of each section of colour A, simply carry the yarn up the side. At the end of each colour B stripe, fasten off and weave in your ends.
- To change the size of your blanket you will need a multiple of 2 stitches for your foundation chain.

STITCHES AND ABBREVIATIONS

Bpdc - Back Post Double Crochet

Ch – Chain

Dc - Double Crochet

Fpdc - Front Post Double Crochet

Hdc - Half Double Crochet

Rpt – Repeat

Sc - Single Crochet

Sk - Skip

Sl St – Slip Stitch

Yo – Yarn Over

PATTERN:

With colour A, Ch 70.

Row 1: Dc in the 4th ch from your hook and in each ch across. Ch 1, turn. (68 sts here and throughout)

Rows 2-3: Hdc in the 1st st, * fpdc around the next st, bpdc around the next st; Rpt from * across to the last st, hdc in the top of the turning chain. Ch 1, turn.

Row 4: Hdc in the 1st st, * fpdc around the next st, bpdc around the next st; Rpt from * across to the last st, hdc in the top of the turning chain. Ch 2, turn.

Row 5: Sc in the next st, *Ch 1, sk the next st, sc in the next st; Rpt from * across. Ch 2, turn.

Rows 6-8: Sk the 1st sc, sc in the next ch-1 sp, *Ch 1, sk the next sc, sc in the next ch-1 sp; Rpt from * across working your final sc into the final ch-2 sp. Ch 2, turn.

Row 9: Sk the 1st sc, sc in the next ch-1 sp, *Ch 1, sk the next sc, sc in the next ch-1 sp; Rpt from * across working your final sc into the final ch-2 sp. At the end of row 9 switch to colour B in the final st. Ch 2, turn.

Rows 10-11: With colour B, Sk the 1st sc, sc in the next ch-1 sp, *Ch 1, sk the next sc, sc in the next ch-1 sp; Rpt from * across working your final sc into the final ch-2 sp. At the end of row 11 switch to colour A in the final st. Ch 2, turn.

Rows 12-21: With colour A, sk the 1st sc, sc in the next ch-1 sp, *Ch 1, sk the next sc, sc in the next ch-1 sp; Rpt from * across working your final sc into the final ch-2 sp. At the end of row 21 switch to colour B in the final st. Ch 2, turn.

Rows 22-23: With colour B, Sk the 1st sc, sc in the next ch-1 sp, *Ch 1, sk the next sc, sc in the next ch-1 sp; Rpt from * across working your final sc into the final ch-2 sp. At the end of row 23 switch to colour A in the final st. Ch 2, turn.

PATTERN CONTINUED:

Rows 24-59: Repeat Rows 12-23 three more times.

Rows 60-64: With colour A, sk the 1st sc, sc in the next ch-1 sp, *Ch 1, sk the next sc, sc in the next ch-1 sp; Rpt from * across working your final sc into the final ch-2 sp. Ch 2, turn.

Row 65: Sk the 1st sc, sc in the next ch-1 sp, *Ch 1, sk the next sc, sc in the next ch-1 sp; Rpt from * across working your final sc into the final ch-2 sp. Ch 3 (Counts as a dc), turn.

Row 66: Dc in the next st and in each st and ch-1 sp across. Ch 1, turn. (Note: at the end of this row ensure that you have a total of 68 sts including your starting ch-3)

Rows 67-69: Hdc in the 1st st, * fpdc around the next st, bpdc around the next st; Rpt from * across to the last st, hdc in the top of the turning chain. Ch 1, turn.

At the end of row 69, fasten off and weave in your ends.

FAUX KNIT COTTAGE BLANKET 

MATERIALS AND INFORMATION

Skill Level: Intermediate

Gauge: 6 sts x 5 rows of pattern = 4 inches

Finished Size: 41 x 53 inches

Yarn: Sweet Snuggles ™ by Loops & Threads ® (100% Polyester; 250 g/8.8 oz; Approx. 109 yds/100 meters). Jumbo (7). Colours Shown: Winter White. You will need 8 balls or about 872 yds in total.

Hook: Size N/P 15 (10.0 mm) Hook. Adjust hook size if necessary to obtain correct gauge.

Notions: Yarn Needle

PATTERN NOTES

- Pattern is written in American English terms.
- Pattern is worked in rows.
- Ch 1 at beginning of row does not count as a stitch.
- This blanket is worked lengthwise (along the long edge).
- Weave in ends as needed.
- To change the size of your blanket you may use any multiple of stitches for your foundation chain.

STITCHES AND ABBREVIATIONS

Blo - Back Loop Only

Ch – Chain

Dc - Double Crochet

Hdc - Half Double Crochet

Hsc – Herringbone Single Crochet (Insert your hook through loop on the front of the post of the previous st, insert your hook into the next stitch, yarn over and draw up a loop, yarn over and draw through all three loops on your hook. Herringbone Single Crochet made.)

Rpt – Repeat

Sc - Single Crochet

Sk - Skip

Sl St – Slip Stitch

Yo – Yarn Over

PATTERN:

Ch 100.

Row 1: Sc in the 2nd ch from your hook, hsc (see "stitches and abbreviations") in the next st and in each st across. Ch 1, turn. (99 sts)

Row 2: Sc in the 1st st, working in the blo across hsc in the next st and in each st across until 1 st remains, working under both loops hsc in the final st. Ch 1, turn.

Rows 3-47: Repeat row 2.

Fasten off, weave in your ends.

To add tassels or not?

This was a question I struggled with for this design! I believe tassels at the end would look amazing (and invite you to try it), however, given my yarn's desire to fray, I opted to not. A simple knotted fringe or twisted fringe would look lovely!

LAVENDER FIELDS BLANKET 

MATERIALS AND INFORMATION

Skill Level: Easy

Gauge: 7 sts x 6 rows of hdc = 4 inches

Finished Size: 46 x 53 inches

Yarn: Sweet Snuggles ™ by Loops & Threads ® (100% Polyester; 250 g/8.8 oz; Approx. 109 yds/100 meters). Jumbo (7). Colour Shown: Lavender. You will need 9 balls or about 981 yds.

Hook: Size N/P 15 (10.0 mm) Hook. Adjust hook size if necessary to obtain correct gauge.

Notions: Yarn Needle

PATTERN NOTES

- Pattern is written in American English terms.
- Pattern is worked in rows.
- Ch 1 at beginning of row does not count as a stitch.
- Ch 2 at beginning of row does not count as a stitch.
- Weave in ends as needed.
- To change the size of your blanket you will need an even number of stitches (Multiple of 2) for your foundation chain.

STITCHES AND ABBREVIATIONS

Bpdc - Back Post Double Crochet

Ch – Chain

Dc - Double Crochet

Hdc - Half Double Crochet

Rpt – Repeat

Sc - Single Crochet

Sk - Skip

Sl St – Slip Stitch

Yo – Yarn Over

PATTERN:

Ch 70

Row 1: Hdc in the 2nd ch from your hook and in each st across. Ch 1, turn. (69 sts here and throughout)

Row 2: Hdc in the 1st st and in each st across. Ch 1, turn.

Row 3: Hdc in the 1st st and in each st across. Ch 2 (does not count as a st), turn.

Row 4: Dc in the 1st st and in each st across. Ch 1, turn.

Row 5: Hdc in the 1st st, *fpdc in the next st, bpdc in the next st; Rpt from * across ending with a hdc in the final st. Ch 1, turn.

Rows 6-7: Hdc in the 1st st and in each st across. Ch 1, turn.

Row 8: Hdc in the 1st st and in each st across. Ch 2 (does not count as a st), turn.

Rows 9 - 58: Repeat rows 4-8 for a total of 10 more times.

Fasten off, weave in your ends.

Did you know?

All of the crochet blankets in this book are reversible! Each blanket is the same front and back and features texture on both sides!

SIMPLY WAFFLES BLANKET

MATERIALS AND INFORMATION

Skill Level: Intermediate

Gauge: 7 sts x 4 rows of pattern = 4 inches

Finished Size: 46 x 57 inches

Yarn: Sweet Snuggles ™ by Loops & Threads ® (100% Polyester; 250 g/8.8 oz; Approx. 109 yds/100 meters). Jumbo (7). Colours Shown: Chalk Blue. You will need 10 balls or about 1090 yds in total.

Hook: Size N/P 15 (10.0 mm) Hook. Adjust hook size if necessary to obtain correct gauge.

Notions: Yarn Needle

PATTERN NOTES

- Pattern is written in American English terms.
- Pattern is worked in rows.
- Ch 1 at beginning of row does not count as a stitch.
- Ch 2 at beginning of row does not count as a stitch.
- Ch 3 at beginning of row counts as a double crochet stitch.
- Weave in ends as needed.
- To change the size of your blanket you will need a multiple of 3 stitches, plus 2 more stitches for your foundation chain.

STITCHES AND ABBREVIATIONS

Bpdc - Back Post Double Crochet

Ch – Chain

Dc - Double Crochet

Fpdc - Front Post Double Crochet

Hdc - Half Double Crochet

Rpt – Repeat

Sc - Single Crochet

Sk - Skip

Sl St – Slip Stitch

Yo – Yarn Over

PATTERN:

Ch 71.

Row 1: Dc in the 3rd ch from your hook and in each ch across. Ch 2, turn. (69 sts here and throughout)

Row 2: Dc in 1st st, *fpdc around post of the next st, dc in each of the next 2 sts, repeat from until 2 sts remain, fpdc around post of the next st, dc in the final st. Ch 2, turn.

Row 3: Dc in each of the 1st 2 sts, *fpdc around post of each of the next 2 sts, dc in the next st; repeat from * until 1 st remains, dc in the final st. Ch 2, turn.

Rows 4-53: Repeat rows 2 and 3. At the end of row 53, ch 1, turn.

Continued...

PATTERN CONTINUED:

Edging (Worked in rounds):

Rnd 1: Hdc in the 1st st and in each st across to the final st, work 3 hdc in the corner st, evenly work 73 hdc along the rough edge to the next corner, work 3 hdc in the corner, hdc in each st across to the next corner, work 3 hdc in the corner st, evenly work 73 hdc along the final rough edge to the final corner, 2 hdc in the final corner. Join with a sl st in the top of the 1st st. (292 sts)

NOTE: You may adjust the number of stitches you work along the rough edge if needed. Simply make note of the number of stitches worked and be sure to work the same number on the opposite side.

Fasten off, weave in your ends.

STUDIO BLANKET

MATERIALS AND INFORMATION

Skill Level: Easy

Gauge: 6 sts x 4 rows of pattern = 4 inches

Finished Size: 46 x 58 inches

Yarn: Sweet Snuggles ™ by Loops & Threads ® (100% Polyester; 250 g/8.8 oz; Approx. 109 yds/100 meters). Jumbo (7). Colour Shown: Fog. You will need 12 balls or about 1300 yds.

Hook: Size N/P 15 (10.0 mm) Hook. Adjust hook size if necessary to obtain correct gauge.

Notions: Yarn Needle

PATTERN NOTES

- Pattern is written in American English terms.
- Pattern is worked in rows.
- Ch 1 at beginning of row does not count as a stitch.
- Ch 2 at beginning of row does not count as a stitch.
- Ch 3 at beginning of row counts as a double crochet stitch.
- Weave in ends as needed.
- To change the size of your blanket you will need an even number of stitches (Multiple of 2) for your foundation chain.

STITCHES AND ABBREVIATIONS

Bpdc - Back Post Double Crochet

Ch – Chain

Dc - Double Crochet

Fpdc - Front Post Double Crochet

Hdc - Half Double Crochet

Rpt – Repeat

Sc - Single Crochet

Sk - Skip

Sl St – Slip Stitch

Yo – Yarn Over

PATTERN:

Ch 70

Row 1: Sc in the 2nd ch from your hook and in each st across. Ch 3, turn. (69 sts here and throughout)

Row 2: Dc in the next st and in each st across. Ch 1, turn.

Row 3: Hdc in the 1st st, * fpdc around the next st, bpdc around the next st; Rpt from * across to the last st, hdc in the top of the turning chain. Ch 1, turn.

Rows 4 - 52: Repeat row 3.

Row 53: Sc in the 1st st and in each st across. Ch 1, turn.

Continued...

PATTERN CONTINUED:

Edging (Worked in rounds):

Rnd 1: Sc in the 1st st and in each st across to the final st, work 3 sc in the corner st, evenly work 73 sc along the rough edge to the next corner, work 3 sc in the corner, sc in each st across to the next corner, work 3 sc in the corner st, evenly work 73 sc along the final rough edge to the final corner, 2 sc in the final corner. Join with a sl st in the top of the 1st st. Do not turn. (292 sts)

NOTE: You may adjust the number of stitches you work along the rough edge if needed. Simply make note of the number of stitches worked and be sure to work the same number on the opposite side.

Rnd 2: Sc in the same st as joining and in each st around, working 3 sc in each of the four corner sts. Join with a sl st in the 1st st. (300 sts)

Fasten off, weave in your ends.

STITCH ABBREVIATIONS AND CHARTS

US to UK Stitch Conversion

US TERM	UK TERM
CHAIN (CH)	CHAIN (CH)
SLIP STITCH (SL ST)	SLIP STITCH (SL ST)
SINGLE CROCHET (SC)	DOUBLE CROCHET (DC)
SINGLE CROCHET TWO TOGETHER (SC2TOG)	DOUBLE CROCHET TWO TOGETHER (DC2TOG)
HALF DOUBLE CROCHET (HDC)	HALF TREBLE (HTR)
DOUBLE CROCHET (DC)	TREBLE (TR)
HALF TREBLE (HTR)	HALF DOUBLE TREBLE (HDTR)
TREBLE/TRIPLE (TR)	DOUBLE TREBLE (DTR)

Yarn Weight Conversion Chart

US TERM	UK TERM	AU TERM	SYMBOL
JUMBO	ROVING	20 PLY	7 JUMBO
SUPER BULKY	SUPER CHUNKY	16 PLY	6 SUPER BULKY
BULKY	CHUNKY	12 PLY	5 BULKY
WORSTED WEIGHT	ARAN	10 PLY	4 MEDIUM
LIGHT WORSTED	DK (DOUBLE KNITTING)	8 PLY	3 LIGHT
SPORT WEIGHT	SPORT WEIGHT	5 PLY	2 FINE
FINGERING OR SOCK WEIGHT	4 PLY OR SOCK WEIGHT	4 PLY OR SOCK WEIGHT	1 SUPER FINE
FINGERING OR SOCK WEIGHT	3 PLY OR BABY	3 PLY	1 SUPER FINE
LACE WEIGHT	2 PLY OR LACE WEIGHT	1-3 PLY	0 LACE

Crochet Hook Conversion Chart

MILLIMETER SIZE	US SIZE
2.25mm	B/1
2.5mm	--
2.75mm	C/2
3mm	D
3.25 mm	D/3
3.5mm	E/4
3.75mm	F/5
4mm	G/6
4.5mm	7
5mm	H/8
5.5mm	I/9
6mm	J/10
6.5mm	K/10.5
7mm	--
8mm	L/11
10mm	N/P/15
15mm	P/Q

Abbreviation Chart

ABBREVIATION	DESCRIPTION
BPDC	BACK POST DOUBLE CROCHET
CH	CHAIN STITCH
CH-SP	CHAIN SPACE
DC	DOUBLE CROCHET
FPDC	FRONT POST DOUBLE CROCHET
HDC	HALF DOUBLE CROCHET
RPT	REPEAT
SC	SINGLE CROCHET
SC2TOG	SINGLE CROCHET TWO STITCHES TOGETHER
SK	SKIP
SL ST	SLIP STITCH
SP	SPACE
ST	STITCH
STS	STITCHES
YO	YARN OVER
*	REPEAT THE INSTRUCTIONS FOLLOWING THE SINGLE ASTERISK AS DIRECTED

NOTES

About the author

Sarah Thompson has been designing crochet patterns since 2018. It wasn't until 2020 that she left her day job to design full-time. She works under the name Rich Textures Crochet, where her original crochet patterns focus on the beauty of textured stitches. She continues to inspire many in the art of crochet. She lives in Ontario, Canada, with her husband, their children, dogs, hamster and bunny. Find her free crochet patterns at richtexturescrochet.com and video tutorials on YouTube @RichTexturesCrochet

www.ingramcontent.com/pod-product-compliance
Lightning Source LLC
Chambersburg PA
CBHW042053030726
47599CB00019B/2477